THE HOMESTEADER

THE HOMESTEADER

A. Van Jordan

UNICORN PRESS

GREENSBORO 2013

First printing

Library of Congress Cataloging-in-Publication Data

Jordan, A. Van.
   [Poems. Selections]
   The Homesteader / A. Van Jordan. —First edition.
   pages. cm. Poems.

   ISBN 978-0-87775-973-7 (Paperback)
   ISBN 978-0-87775-974-4 (Hardback)

   1. Title.
PS 3610.O654 H66 2013   811'.6—dc23   2012-044811

∞
This book is printed on Mohawk Superfine, which is acid-
free and meets ANSI standards for archival permanence.

Unicorn Press
1212 Grove Street
Greensboro, NC 27403

www.unicorn-press.org

For Oscar Micheaux

FADE IN: INTERIOR—TRAIN—1902

Pullman Porter OSCAR MICHEAUX, *while en route to Chicago from Cleveland, overhears passengers talking about homesteading land in South Dakota and Nebraska.*

Silent. I showed a patron to her seat.
She traveled alone, walking behind me.
And though I heard her heels, I held my eyes.
She had nothing to say, just greeted me
With ticket shoved in my palm, intimate
It almost felt, but distant with silence.
Just as one train car leads to another,
So her walk through coach led her to talking
To others about a Rosebud homestead,
A new farming town of Gregory, new
To white men, at least; Lakotas tilled land
There years before. I read of land to claim,
Land to claim for any man man-enough
To make it grow, Negro or white alike.

And I'm a Negro who can make it grow.
Once I got word of what I needed, I
Turned my own train around. I had to know
The joy of owning my own land. My eye
Trained on the future, on territory
North, while other race men were headed south.
I lit out solo to find, own, and be
My future by strong back, tack, and by mouth;
I knew I'd compete elbow to elbow
With white men, but I still needed a wife
To keep me sane lest I sing a lowbrow
Fool's tune: humming *Hmm, hmm, Hmm* through my life.
Now, I need a few nights of heaven here
To live with a woman, pick out our star.

INT. BASEMENT. NATIONAL PENCIL CO. FACTORY,
MILLEDGEVILLE, GA. SATURDAY/SUNDAY,
APRIL 26/27, 1913–DAY

MARY PHAGAN, *13-year-old factory worker, deceased (VO)*

My body's sky; they try to pick a star:
Police ask questions as if, from this far,
I could answer. All I offer lies here.
I'm not resisting or playing coy. Fear
Envelopes the room as much as it filled
My lungs the night all this trouble started.
My eyes look into theirs asking, fighting
To ask, them to keep asking: My sphinxing
Self. If the killer's clues lie between my legs,
I'll act like a cricket, till my body sings.

Photographs speak little of my distrust
Of men: my white slip, knee-high socks. How I
Placed more faith in the father in his eye,
Than all my attempts to avoid men's lust….

LEO FRANK, *manager of the National Pencil Company
in Milledgeville, GA, is on trial for the murder of Mary
Phagan. Frank, Jewish, is accused of the crime, but there's
no forensic evidence linking him to the murder. But the
townspeople and authorities have accused the outsider from
Brooklyn, NY. He waits in jail for another day on trial.*

Of the dangers I avoided of lust,
Of frauds against my case, of witnesses
Without a crime, of lies from men unjust—
What can I say? Is there any defense?

Infinite pleadings, naked offerings,
The tenderness of truth reworked, retold—
The truth of childhood is now abhorring—
The Negroes grow pliant, yielding, controlled,

Folding under threats against their own kin,
In work places, at home; beaten, breathless,
Under hoods at night, the threat trumps the sin,
And now our fate is weighed by the careless.

To hell with any issues around why;
The answer carries too much history.
I just want the past to lie down and die.

EXTERIOR—ON THE ROAD—1913—NIGHT

Believing Leo Frank is innocent, bounty hunter EARL
HIGGINBOTTOM *travels through the Great Plains in horse
and buggy to Milledgeville,* GA, *in search of Mary Phagan's
true killer.*

First, I want the past to lie down and die
While I move ahead and find you: bounty,
Lover, song. I need the whole world to get
Behind me. I need the path to sunset
Lined with prospects not nostalgia. Some day
I'd like to teach myself something new, a
Trade other than binding men, an avenue
To art, to say what I feel, what I knew
Of life. If I can't have love, then no new
Pain can enter these clothes I wear, see?
With no one to lose, no one can lose me.

Like a daguerreotype, my wife lies here,
And her body reminds me she was here,
As the past taunts the present, striking fear.

African American actress and contemporary of Lillian Gish, MADAME SUL-TE-WAN *appeared in many films for Griffith as a maid or mammy figure; she was rarely credited, not even in* Birth of A Nation. *She prepares.*

Real-life scenes strike fear, while past scenes just taunt,
Watching them on screen. Now, I may stumble
But Madame Sul-Te-Wan will never fall.
The metamorphosis was worth the pain.
The anticipation was worth the wait.
In Louisville, Kentucky, life was calm,
If you wanted to live without living.

I needed more; I decided to change:
The name, the home, but I ain't forgot me.
Griffith gives me a job without credit,
No star to hang a name from. Serving up
A plate of homemade pancakes is my role...
No change: I came to play a maid on screen.
It rings clear: Our work on *Birth* brings no love.

Newsreel of D.W. GRIFFITH *in his library at home after the release of his biggest financial success,* Birth of a Nation, *which, like Thomas Dixon's* The Clansman *from which it was adapted, he sees as a "Southern romance," which was the novel's subtitle.*

Birth of a Nation brings a love story
About men and women from bordered soil
During the war, to wide-screen destiny:
The North, it seems, set the country aboil.
While the Klieg-lit south tried to end this feud.
This story kept our focus on lovers,
In times when talking about love rang rude.
Look, see how they stare into each other's
Eyes. Pull in. Close ups bring out emotion,
Brings her moist lips, his tear-filled eyes, their mirth.
They don't want Civil War—just devotion.
Our lovers, like soldiers, rove back and forth.
And when both push passion, pushed to a rest,
Just a touch of sweat slides south, down her breast.

*Front porch of home of Oscar, now homesteading farmer
and Negro novelist. He contemplates his affection for and
relationship with his Scottish neighbor's daughter,* AGNES.

Just a hint of sweat, Agnes, on your breast,
Reminds me now of our night in shadow,
Hiding from your father's gaze. He didn't
Know—or care, seems, coming from Scotland—but
Others lie in wait, North and South, to cut
Our throats, but just to think… no, I shouldn't
Think of a white woman. This puts me through
A spectrum of scrutiny; a real test

For a race man, a real forecast of pain;
To know our life is hard is no riddle.
This may sound foolish, maybe pivotal,
But Negroes and whites, we're just built for strain.

If we had children, though we'd hope they'd thrive,
Desire builds a war they could not survive.

INT. REV. NEWTON MCCRACKEN'S HOME, CHICAGO. APRIL 21, 1910—DAY

Oscar meets and decides to marry ORLEAN MCCRACKEN, *the daughter of a preacher that Oscar sees as an after-church-chicken-dinner-eatin' charlatan. Tensions rise between the father and Oscar.*

Rev. Newton McCracken

To survive this war with my girl's husband,
Between this young man and a man like me,
Orlean needs to choose God for her life.

Between him and a Godly man like me,
Well, a young buck loses every time.
She shares my blood, my home, my dreams; he'll see.

You can't tell me nothin'. Love ain't a crime,
Unless it comes outside church. Husband or not:
A husband's gonna lose every time.

Whether he tries to tell me or not,
I've taken care of her and her mother;
No man can tell me what *needs* and what *ought.*

Keep her in church, and stay out of her ear.
You can't break the laws of God, actin' grown.

Oscar

Man, forget all the laws; we're in love and grown.
Know what's in her prayers, Rev? My hands, my mouth....
Look: Preachers' daughters always get their men,
Even when preachers thump bibles over beds,

Even if the church doesn't say amen;
A preacher's daughter always gets her man.
Like Song of Songs, my left hand holds her head.
Who cares if the church doesn't say amen?
As my right hand embraces her body,
Like Solomon, my left hand holds her head.
And I'll kiss her with the wine of my mouth,
As my right hand embraces her body.
Naked, she comes to me; I'll kiss her mouth
Through the night; like wine, coming, her body.

INT—OFFICE OF GOVERNOR
OF GEORGIA, 1915—DAY

JOHN M. SLATON, *who, after hearing of the trumped-up*
charges against Leo Frank, and after pressure from liberal
groups, decides to commute Frank's sentence down to life in
prison, though he believes he was innocent. Slaton believes it
is better than giving him a death sentence.

Through the night, unrest breaks. How to survive?
A life worth saving, my conscience to calm…
With all on my mind, now, at stake are lives;
Leo Frank's and others lie in the palm

Of my hand, and I have no peace to bring.
That's the problem: Too few consequences
For living wrong. It's now winter, and spring
Is forever coming. Accomplices

To the crime sit on the jury making
Bad decisions, forcing me to play judge.
Georgia is no playground, and tampering
Is beneath my office, but there's a grudge

Growing in the hearts of the townspeople.
Like hands folding into fists, the people.

EXT—MILLEDGEVILLE—1915—
ANONYMOUS—DAY / NIGHT

*African American residents and workers from the National
Pencil Factory of Milledgeville, where the trial is held,
and residents of Marietta, birthplace of Mary Phagan, are
threatened by emerging Klansmen—men calling themselves
the* Knights of Mary Phagan, *emboldened by* Birth of a
Nation—*with the murder of their families and the burning
of their homes if they don't witness against Leo Frank.*

Like hands folding into fists, the people
Came to find justice, came to blame someone.
When man makes mistakes, work to correct them;
Not a clear lesson for any man's life.
Tough love, dear mirror, barked my reflection,
But now is no time for recollection.
Now, in Milledgeville, I fear for my life.
The factory Negroes, and all of 'em,
Get threats all day and all night by someone,
Who appears as no one, hooded people,

Men with guns. All's I know. And men with guns
Run this trial. Frank is a prisoner
But we're all held hostage, we who law shuns
Sleep with our shoes on, while saying a prayer.

INT—FLASHBACK—MICHEAUX HOME—
GREGORY, SD—1912—DAY

*At the urging of her minister father and her family, his
wife, Orlean—after suffering a miscarriage—has left him.
Micheaux makes one last effort to make it on his homestead but
surrenders on this final day, setting out on a period of itinerancy.*

With shoes on feet and prayer on tongue, I drive;
I branch into art from crops with no wife.
Like a face caught off screen, now I'm alive;
I've found my game without wielding a knife.
Though through the lens my eye glints like a knife,
My focus is race to prove I'm alive.
I'm a new Negro; that's how I survive.
Film is my path now, later for a wife.
This ain't one about the dutiful wife,
Or fathers worried their sons won't revive
A South defeated under the North's knife.
This is my work, how I know I'm alive.
This story of a man left by his wife,
Proves a man can choose art over the knife.

I proved man could choose art over the knife
When she asked how much it would cost to make
This "movie thing," what kind of risk involved,
I knew then she would have me plowing fields.
This girl is my past now, not the woman
I once loved. I might be broke but I have
Class, but you can't have class and be cheap. I
Said, "You think Griffith has to deal with this?"
She said, "You ain't Griffith, Negro" as she
Walked out the sod-house door. And I watched as
Her blurred figure burned off the horizon

Faster than my name blew free from her lips.
An apparition in my mind now, but
I still see her...though, I must look ahead.

INT—HOTEL ROOM, CHICAGO—JUNE 1913—DAY

Later, mid-year, Oscar's loneliness is getting the better of him. He's still trying to make sense of what happened in his marriage, and he's still determined to make it as a writer.

Looking ahead pushes the past deeper
Inside my pocket: memories, jangling
Like loose change but diminishing,
Day in and day out, as I try to figure
Out what comes next. The sky won't predict days
Of prosperity, days of loss, but I
Study. I watch. Take the Epsom Derby:
A woman stepped out in front of the King's
Horse; she was trampled to death. She was a
Suffragist, Emily Davison. Now,
I respect her death, like taking a vow,
She died trying to make change, in her way,
Which baffles the spectators, watching from
The stands. She died to keep from eating crumbs.

Others die complacent, eating crumbs from
hands starving them. Most people don't think, see;
they figure she must've been confused, she
must've been trying to take something from
or attach something, a flag, to the horse.
But, no, maybe she just wanted to push
Others to take action, to chart a course
To make others ask why, you know, to flush
Out the rhetoric, the philosophy.
It's hard to find an act more pure than death.
It's hard to find a message more clear. Death
Always appears on the set of our lives
In the background, still, urging us to live—
Spiriting us all on like family.

All of the dead ascend to family,
And we take note of our lives, checking in
To see how we're doing with life, what's been
At the center of our hearts. The daily
Jabs at others and their politics seem
Smaller in light of loss, in the wake of
Losing my wife, even this feels extreme—
As if I'm in mourning, though I lost love.
She was with child, double loss, from which there
Was no coming back. Orlean and I knew
Our baby was our last chance to declare
Peace between her father and me. So few
Chances in this world to share a twin bill:
One's love to find, one's calling to fulfill.

But what else should we try to fulfill? Work
And love. What else is out there? Nothing worth
Pursuing. I've seen men sidetracked by less,
Believing life's a trick, when it's a test
Of will. It's a world filled with temptation.
It's a world of adult situations.
It's up to me to figure out the path,
Whether with a wife or not, the road's wrath
Awaits me. Leaving South Dakota was
A blessing I didn't see because
I couldn't hear the message calling out
For me to stop acting a knockabout.
Where are the voices of expectation?
Of people in action? Their vibration?

I need the vibration of people in
Action, not those chewing their cud out west,
But the verve of the east coast: a Brooklyn
Or Harlem, D.C., but no more Midwest
Than Chicago, for sure, but skyscrapers
And crowds, for sure, for sure. I need Negroes
As real race men, not breeders but readers—
And minds adrift like archipelagoes,
Exploring beyond the backs of their hands.
Whenever the sun breaks, peering through clouds,
Swords of light falling through a window, lands
Coming to life—an empty street, a crowd,
Or a field of corn from my past—the strand
Of a story unfolds beneath my hands.

As the story unfolds beneath my hands,
Black stones lift from the ground within my mind,
Not clearing my path, but stones left behind
To show others the way. There are few strands
Of experience to pass on in film.
Those floating around are not sent for me.
Once I get started, I'll clear the debris
From the road; the path gets fired in the kiln.
But I'm getting ahead of myself. I'm
Still learning my way, and, to be fair, white
Men have helped to shape how I see the light
Bend through a doorway for effect, and I'm
Grateful for the gesture, though they did not
Think that I'd ever fully work this knot.

But here I am, working, like it or not,
And a Negro world is building before
Me. If not used, a man's talents dry rot,
Whether with work or with women, for sure;
If I don't take care of the blessing, I'll
Lose it. Why not take a chance to see what
I can do now with no wife or child while
I only have one mission left, uncut
By lust or love? Even the prophet in
The Valley of Dry Bones could bring to life
Those who once lived. So why should life wear thin
For those who believe but don't have a wife?
Can't wait on love to swing into action.
I look outside, search, find new attractions.

INT—JAILHOUSE, MILLEDGEVILLE, GA—1915—NIGHT

Leo Frank. His last night in jail after the verdict. Later tonight, a group of men calling themselves The Knights of Mary Phagan *will break him out of jail, drag him to Marietta, and hang him, publicly. He will be the first and only Jewish American, on record, to suffer this horror. Leo thinks about the pain and suffering the trial has caused his wife.*

I see you when I look outside, daily,
Even when you're not there. You stand in front
Of me, finding a smile through bad news: I'm
Not coming home. You know I need your smile.
Without freedom to walk through town, I know
You live in prison, too. Yours seems harder
To define than stone, than iron bars; yours
Moves without walls around all corners; yours
Seeks some peace to tamp it down. It's harder
To rake a cup against no bars, you know,
But you find a way to make noise. No smile
Comes when I think of you not smiling. I'm
Left wringing my hands; you keep up the front!
I see you when I look outside, daily.

Orlean dies from being trampled by a horse on her way to church. After being brought to a Whites Only hospital in Chicago, she was refused admittance and died en route to St. Lukes, a hospital that admitted Negroes. Oscar's financial problems have increased after losing the homestead. From his train car, he ruminates on the past few years, embattled with the McCrackens. He begins looking for other ways, including his novels and making film, to not only make a living, but also to make an impact on the public consciousness. In the mean time, he's also trying to deal with loneliness.

Daily, I look outside and I see hell.
You think it's sad? A man with no woman?
Try life as a man with no money. Now
There's a sad story. I can't think sweetheart
When I'm sinking in debt, but, I confess:
Orlean's handwriting was the prettiest
I had ever seen, but film's my wife now.
I left her letters behind to find my-
Self. Screen couples show an Every Man
Loving an Every Woman. I mold
Stand-ins for us, sculptures looking the part,
But, being an artist in need of love,
My hammer shattered us like a sculpture.
Dear Orlean, this is our story to tell.

MONTAGE/INT/EXT—MOVIE HOUSES—NIGHT—
MILLEDGEVILLE...MARIETTA...CLEAVELAND...
CHICAGO...KANSAS CITY...MOBILE...LITTLE
ROCK...AND MANY MORE—1915—ANONYMOUS

African Americans all over America go to the movies, as they have been since before the Lincoln Picture Company started releasing Race Films in 1913. But they must deal with Jim Crow laws and sit in "Nigger Heaven," the balcony.

Men and women have some stories to tell.
Most men and women have stories to tell.
Life be pourin' out 'em, like trains skippin' off rails.

Movies tell stories I wish I could live.
Heroes say what I can't, but *still* get to live.
But I'd play the villain, given one chance to live.

I go to movies by foot, bus, or train.
I get across town by foot, bus, or train.
Man, all kinds of travel, brakes one helluva strain.

When the hero wants to sleep with a girl,
He'll deep-sea dive just to find her a pearl.
Whatever it takes, he says, to sleep with the girl.

At the movies, my arm falls over her shoulder.
At the movies, we keep our minds on each other.

Earl Higginbottom, on the trail of JIM CONLEY, *whom he
believes to be Phagan's killer, has arrived in the state of
Georgia. His first night there, like every night alone, brings
his mind to his deceased wife,* HATTIE. *He decides to go to a
movie to clear his head.*

Even at a movie, I keep my mind
On my wife. I forget war, focus on
What I loved before talk of secession:
Hattie, my wife, is all my head can find.

If hands hold memories, mine remember her
Feet soaking in water basins: my hands
Dry her toes. I surrender: her finger
Parts my hair when she oils my scalp. Man's
Every morning dims to less certain
With every night's regret. I see vestiges
Of battle fields, fallen soldiers, women
Of whose fates I dare not speak, shortages

Of food, of work, and, still, men want to fight;
Like mine, their shadows cast from fallen light.

INT. NEW YORK PENN STATION—DAY, AUGUST 18, 1915, 6 A.M.

The Crescent Star enters New York's Penn Station from
Atlanta, transporting the body of Leo Frank. The New York
Times reports a "Negro sophisticate" was in the crowd…Oscar.

Their shadows are cast from the light falling
Through the windows, the way shadows crawl and
Float, all at once. The windows resist and
Aid the gaze of crowds more than sun streaming

Through, but the shadows persist against light
Setting, as if awaiting an actor
To come forward, hit his mark. An actor
However, would enjoy life in the light.

Leo Frank has no voice to play his role,
To move from the shadows. Who plays his role?
The body is already at rest. What
More can a corpse do beyond continue

As totem? What can a memory do?
The body is already at rest. What?

INT—HARLEM HOTEL ROOM—
AUGUST 18, 1915—NIGHT

Oscar was in Georgia and sat in on the Frank v. State *trial.*
He believes Griffith's Birth of a Nation, *released to success*
just before the verdict, had influence on these events. He tells
others his opinion.

Their bodies already lie at rest. What,
If anything, could Leo Frank and
Mary Phagan do to any man? And
I mean dead or alive. I'm asking what

Does a mob think happens if a man is
Jew or Negro in a community
Of white? I can't change a community,
But seek dignity, capital; life is

Changing daily. Film has great influence,
Maybe more than money itself. I need
To stop farming, start sowing film. I need
To stop dreaming, start having influence

On lives, not just Negroes but on whites, too.
Like taxes, we all pay when death comes due.

INT—OFFICES OF LINCOLN FILM COMPANY—
LOS ANGELES—1918—DAY

NOBLE JOHNSON, *co-founder of Lincoln Film Company with
his brother George, agrees to work with Oscar to help distribute
and promote his films. The deal falls through, though.
Oscar goes on to make and distribute his own film under the
Micheaux Film and Book Company out of Sioux City.*

Listen, after these new taxes are paid,
After the snow melts over the country,
After the parties, after the rent gets paid,
After, for once, we feel like one country,

After the crops are picked and meted out.
I want people to see our lives as lives
Not sharecroppers, not rations or handouts,
Not stumps to serve, but as heroes—real lives.

So open the main floor to Negroes. Yes,
Open the curtain and reveal the screen.
I want them to laugh, cry, quarrel, and, yes,
Make love after seeing our films on screen.

You can live like a saint but have nothing.
Why not raise hell? What's to be lost?...Nothing.

JIM CONLEY, *three years later and many years after that, is constantly questioned about the Leo Frank v. Mary Phagan trial.*

I knowed hell and I had nothin' to lose,
But I been tellin' 'em I had nothin'
To do with no Mary Phagan; now, I
Told the courts I helped Mr Frank with her,
But I *had* to say, what they said to say.
That's jus' how it goes: Me or him. The world
Ain't studyin' ole Jim Conley; the world
Care about the girl 'cause she white; all they say
Is our children ain't safe, meaning like her,
Young white girls. Man, they aint talking 'bout my
Children. They threatens to kill mines. Nothin'
Left to give; I got nothin' left to lose.

Say, what you will, 'bout my story changin',
I sleeps in peace, and thas not just dreamin.'

INSERT SHOT: THE CHICAGO DEFENDER:
HEADLINE: *"WOMAN RAPED AND LYNCHED BY MOB
OF SOUTHERN WHITE MEN."* DECEMBER 18, 1919

CORDELIA & ARCH STEVENSON *are attacked in their sleep
after a white farmer accuses their son of setting fire to his barn.
Their son had not been to town for months.*

To slumber Wednesday night, at peace, dreaming;
To wake to men invading their cabin,
Breaking down the door, knocking first to fool
Cordelia and Arch to think they had guests;
To barge in, hooded, armed, and looking, (they
Say) for her "no 'count" son, finding her there
In bed clothes, husband Arch, in his longjohns,
Shotguns now to his head, he runs to town
For help. No law man, no race man aided
Him. Cordelia, stripped naked, dragged out
To Mobile & Ohio Railroad tracks,
"Maltreated," evidence of men left on
Her body, her body left there hanging
By hands unknown until Friday morning.

INT: FLASHBACK—ATLANTA HOTEL ROOM—
1915—DAY

*Oscar reads the verdict for and sentencing of Leo Frank. He
is disturbed by the Negro "witnesses" that testified against
Frank. He sees them as traitors not just to their race, but also
to race relations with Jews. This sticks with him as he begins
to write and to think about film.*

Boot blacks. Scared maids. Unknown hands on Sunday
Mornings in churchgoer's pockets. I tire
Of ignorant Negroes and hate their fears
More, some days, than the whites threatening them.
The act of lynching Frank, reading Monday
Morning how, "race men" witnessed against fire
Threats, makes me wonder: Don't they own guns? Years
Of threats, lynchings, and rape, and torn from limb

To limb, and they can't see one tree leads to
Another? What did they expect? To start
Living free? Griffith set us back 50
Years, and these witnesses also played roles.
Meaning they need hero roles to witness.
Set clocks 50 years ahead, starting now.

MONTAGE—INT/OSCAR MICHEAUX'S MIND—
1915-1918—DAY/NIGHT

Growing tired of the emboldened responses to Griffith's
Birth of a Nation *and the violence in the wake of the Leo
Frank trial, Oscar realizes he needs a new medium to reach
the public: film. He sees the affect film has on the psyche and
behavior of people, so he embarks on a quest to learn this
new art form. He begins by deciding to adapt his roman à
clef,* The Homesteader, *to the screen.*

Starting now, focused, I see through a lens
All the life I've blurred in my head, chambers
Underground in my mind, I now explore.
When two figures come together to share
Space, find a way to frame their bodies to
Express the love or distance between them…
To compose the movement of a woman
Taking stairs, presents a problem: Women
In motion, show graceful intent. For them,
Walking is art, yes, crossing their legs, too,
While sitting, reading a book, is art. Share
This space with a man, and now you explore
A whole new problem: Loading this chamber
With both, challenges and sharpens the lens.

Sharpen the focus in your lens, and you
Sharpen your view of the world; you can see
How people inhabit space in their lives,
How the skin of Negroes and whites both play
With light, how both reflect from within—light.
How often does one stop to notice this
In the course of one's day? How often do
We think of what shadows and the light do
Together in a space in the world? This
Alone would slow down a day, watching light.
This alone would invite one out to play.
This alone would allow, into your life,
Others. But, no, in life one rarely sees
How light bounces off someone back to you?

As the light bounces back and as the shot
Composes the light and as the gesture
From the actor's hand moves and as rain
Falls on the set fortuitously, saving
A day when we thought we'd have to create
Our own storm, and as we come to understand
How all these elements work, we learn to make
Film. We learn to adapt to the things we make.
Any farmer can tell you, *Understand
The land and you'll sow*. But film can create
The land, the mood of the sky, it can save
The union; if need be, it brings the rain,
It brings sun, it brings both in one gesture,
If need be. It brings life in just one shot.

In just one shot, I could offer a kiss
From a man crossing a room from the left
Of the screen, which offers ease on the eyes
As opposed to his crossing from the right
Or from the bottom up into the frame.
I never thought about how important
The line of vision was in one's daily
Routine. I walk outside and stare daily.
First, I look at the feet, and the import
Of this comes from understanding the frame:
You can create character with the right
Shoes, a woman's arched foot—both draw eyes;
Start there and she's sexy. There's little left
To say. Pull in for the close up, the kiss.

Pull in. Time for the close up: the money.
People give to film like no other art
Or charity I've seen. I imagine
It's for selfish reasons: Everyone wants
Their name in lights, their hand in making
Some howling beautiful thing, the power
To bring women to tears and men to knees
With a flash of powder, a face framed, a knee
Exposed from beneath a dress. The power
Of film, the love of the public, to make
The public love you, feeds the many wants
Of others and offers love back. Image
After image comes down to bringing art
To those in need. And I need their money.

I need money to get started. Novels
Call for sweat and some imagination.
Finding time to write was the biggest block,
But film calls for cash and bodies to work
With me. I like having workers and I
Like having money, so this just suits me
Fine. And I'll give them quality, too. Film
Costs too much to make any junk. My film
Needs to show all sides of the Negro. My
Idea for the screen needs to inspire. I'm
The man I've never seen on screen: I work,
I think, I create, I love. There's no block
Of wood we're carved from. Imagination
Can't cast me on screen. I'm old. I'm novel.

I'll cast characters from *The Homesteader*,
And offer the public a new Negro
To consider. No more blackface sambos;
No more mammies without lives, without homes
Of their own. Who wants to see, all at once,
As if asleep, a woman or man act
As if their souls were out of work and their
Bodies were just hired? This ghost of theirs
Dies on screen at my hand. People will act
Like people whose souls you can knock on, once
I get the camera. The setting? A home
Or field, classroom or bedroom—no sambos
Or mammies allowed. Just real-life Negroes,
Starting now, on screen, a real homesteader.

Starting now, the film we've all been waiting
With held breath to see. *The Homesteader*, film
By Oscar Micheaux. The film debuted at
Eighth Colored Regiment Armory at
8 PM, 35th and Forest streets,
Chicago. Film of marriage and deceit,
Film on which he bet the farm, literally;
Film against church, against hate, against lust
And fate; film of boot straps and pulling, back
Bones and standing upright; film with lines wrapped
Around the block; film in eight reels, first for
Race films; a film so good, tickets sold for
10 cents more; a film with the word niggah,'
But used, this time, by us on screen with hugs.

CUT TO: EXT—MAIN ST—
MILLEDGEVILLE—1919—DAY

Earl Higginbottom catches up with Jim Conley. Thinking
he will bring the man to confess, he soon realizes Conley is
a lost cause and probably not only not smart enough to have
gotten away with the crime, but also that Conley is living
an imprisonment of sorts, anyway. Earl sees Conley as a bad
vaudeville act in black face, except Conley is real.

Used to a life without hugs, not even
From his own kind, Conley is the saddest
Negro I've ever met born in freedom.
Made *me* feel like a man without freedom.
The Phrenologist Coon seemed the saddest
Amos & Andy skit I'd seen, even
Though they wrote it, but now I live it,
Talking to this Negro. I can tell *What's*
In his head by what's in his pocket: no—
Thing. He's empty. A glass to fill up. No,
He lives emptied out; he's to live out what
They want. Unlike him, as a boy, dammit,
I was a man. But I stood up when held
Down; though, when on hard times, I still was held.

INT/EXT—1919

Sprit of Mary Phagan, 13-year-old factory worker (VO)

Mama says you have to fall on hard times
To know how to live; she says I don't know
How hard life bears down on adults, "Damn near
Will kill ya just to live," she says. No doubt,
Mama. I lie in evidence of truth.
I believe her sayings now, but I can't
Trust the John Keats poem from my lessons:
"A thing of beauty is a joy for ever..."; I
Would believe Mr. Keats, but I think he
Died three years after he wrote the poem?
So fo...fo..."For ever?" my voice stutters.
You see, I don't exist; youth is fleeting,
More a puzzle than "a joy," Mr. Keats.
I ponder your poem even in death....

*Spirit of Oscar Micheaux. After a long career as one of
the most successful independent filmmakers of all time,
approximately 40 films from 1919-1948, Oscar dies March
25, 1951, of a heart attack while on a business trip in
Charlotte, NC. His body is interred in Great Bend, KS. (VO)*

Even in death—Hollywood's star-lined streets,
Emblazoned with money and all green lights,
With handshakes and the smiles and the gold streets
Of studios spot-lit and the dim lights
Of front offices— I'd make films in streets.
I'm free: My life was always dreamed in lights;
And now, I've shared ideas in many streets;
As you walk them, watch my labor through light.

What more can I make of a well-wrought life?
As Yeats said, "I spread my dreams under your feet."
And maybe one day, I will have a star
On Hollywood Blvd, and the star
Will hold my dream, which will lie at your feet
At night, my lonely gift, my work, my life....

Earl Higginbottom, having given up the bounty hunting
trade, moves to Chicago to work in the steel mills. Tonight,
he attends the premier of The Homesteader. *(VO)*

Night: In a city under the North Star,
He stops. He's both in delight and dismay,
To watch not a single painted blackface,
The face he faced with horror on his own.

All he knew is now history. Ticket
Stubs sit in hands of the Negro patrons:
Proof of collaboration never seen
First hand, between a race man and a dream.

What a surprise! A film by a Pullman!
And scenes, never seen, come in an array
Of voices, lighting a path to a seat
Like ushers to a future, lighting a
City with farmers wearing spit-shined shoes;
Farmers from Midwest farms travel by train;

By train the bent-back sharecroppers come, too.
They come to Chicago to see, on screen,
Themselves in a different light, no dis-
Grace, just the scent of hard work wafting to
Release in the projector's glow, the glow
Releasing some maids, drivers, and bootblacks;

Small songs of faith from bounty hunters' hearts,
The quiet songs heard only in the bed-
Room at the end of a long trail. Tonight

The music made on farms will rise up from
Streets: Detroit, Cleveland, Kansas City and
Cities alike. Who knows from where our next
Hero hails, but know tonight patrons sit
Silently—not to show you to your seats.

FADE OUT

A. Van Jordan is the author of four collections: *Rise*, which won the PEN / Oakland Josephine Miles Award (Tia Chucha Press, 2001); *M-A-C-N-O-L-I-A* (2005), which was listed as one of the Best Books of 2005 by *The London Times*; *Quantum Lyrics* (2007); and *The Cineaste* (2013), W.W. Norton & Co. Jordan has been awarded a Whiting Writers Award, an Anisfield-Wolf Book Award, and a Pushcart Prize. He is a recipient of a John Simon Guggenheim Fellowship, and a United States Artists Williams Fellowship. He is a Professor in the Department of English at the University of Michigan, and teaches in the MFA Program for Writers at Warren Wilson College.

Text and titles printed in Fournier.
Cover and text designed by Andrew Saulters.

The author signed 26 hardbound copies,
lettered A through z. An additional 100
hardbound copies and 375 bound in paper
were produced by Unicorn Press.